with the dogstar as my witness

with the dogstar as my witness

POEMS BY JOHN FRY

ORISON
BOOKS

Orison Books
PO Box 8385
Asheville, NC 28814
www.orisonbooks.com

ISBN 978-1-949039-20-7

Distributed to the trade by Itasca Books.
1 (800) 901-3480 / orders@itascabooks.com
www.itascabooks.com

Manufactured in the U.S.A.

Cover art: "Cathedral" (jacquard tapestry). Copyright © 2013 by Kiki Smith.
Used by permission of Pace Gallery.

ORISON
BOOKS

CONTENTS

nightwalk

Vigils

nightwalk

Lauds

Acknowledgments

Grateful acknowledgement is made to the publications in which the following poems appeared, sometimes in earlier versions:

Alice Blue Review: "diptych (his hairshirt)," "not-psalm 121"

Bellingham Review: "debris field [in the agony of]"

Blackbird: "wilderness rose as incense"

Borderlands: "debris field [before the world darkened]"

Boxcar Poetry Review: "wonder thicket"

Connotation Press: "you ghost in the logos"

Colorado Review: "as Samuel in the temple"

The Cresset: "true north," "credo [say I am]"

Denver Quarterly: "[now that we're lost at last]"

Ink & Letters: "as Lazarus risen like a blossom from bone," "as the woman who grasped the hem of his garment"

Jam Tarts: "I blew the candle out"

Konundrum Engine Literary Review: "how do you explain it," "torn from a book of what happened"

The Laurel Review: "as Mary after the eclipse of her radiance threshold," "wrecked, solitary, there"

MARY: A Journal of New Writing: "[roads end where only trees greet them]"

The Offending Adam: "every time you wish the sky was something happening to your heart," "soul, paraphrased," "there are four angels standing at the four corners of the earth"

Pebble Lake Review: "as Judas fleeing from the storm in his marrow"

Ruminate: "antiphon (preacher's son)," "antiphon (gnostic stranger)," "antiphon (queer angel)," "breath on a coal," "debris field [& was this also given]," "[now I ache at the strange]"

Switchback: "pilgrim"

Third Coast: "update after the possession"

This Spectral Evidence: "by the light of no moon"

Tupelo Quarterly: "as Eve, remembering Eden"

Water~Stone Review: "approximately never," "as Jonah, hours into the third night, wondered"

West Branch: "[open my heart for the night, it's empty]," "[tucked in the notch of my fossil-bones]," "[through leaves which naturally dizzied &]"

Whale Road Review: "after"

The poem "credo [like a preacher's son]" appeared in the chapbook *silt will swirl* (NewBorder, 2012).

A cloud of witnesses surrounds this breviary, and nothing gives me greater joy than to acknowledge the depth of what I owe to some of them:

Thank you to my teachers during my Carolina sojourn at Davidson College and my homecoming to Tejas at Texas State University. Cynthia Lewis, for fostering my love of George Herbert and Gerard Manley Hopkins. Gail Gibson, for shaping me into the medievalist I've become and for the gifts of Chaucer, Margery Kempe, and Julian of Norwich. Karl Plank, for seeing beyond the near failure of a struggling undergraduate and, years later, your faith in what this book could be. Alan Michael

Parker, for teaching me that a poetry incapable of praise is one incapable of parsing pain. Kathleen Peirce, for showing me how to find where the edges of things are, that poetry is what passes through them, and how to make a life out of this listening. Cyrus Cassells, for giving the soul a singing path I've tried to follow here and for encouraging me to craft my own alphabet of the sacred.

For the light of their examples on/off the page, their friendship, and their belief in this work, thank you to Kazim Ali, Sheila Black, Shiloh Booker, J. Scott Brownlee, Aaron Deutsch, Jill Alexander Essbaum, Carolyn Forché, Tracy Leigh Henry, Jimmy Hsu, Kimberly Johnson, Julie Kantor, Katelin Kelly, James Knippen, Sequoia Maner, Paula Mendoza, Rachel Moritz, Stephanie Motz (*requiescat in pace*, dear friend, te extraño), Amy Newman, Emmy Pérez, Jo Reyes-Boitel, ire'ne lara silva, Luisa Muradyan Tannahill, Brian Teare, Julia Walsh, Kerri Webster, and Andrew Wessels.

My kith, my kin: Blair Breitreiter, sister from another mother, since the fourth grade, now and forever. Michael Garza, circa Corpus Christi, where we read Jorie Graham on the couch of the Lotus Cup and danced in the heaven of the Velvet Room, for the ongoing conversation. Matt Talbert, brother and girlfriend, so much tears and so much laughter. Julie Ruble, providential interlocutor, who met me exactly where I was, who still walks beside. Katherine Sorrell, compañera across the world whether the streets have names or not.

Thank you, Luke Hankins, for giving this peregrine book the best home I could hope to imagine, and for hearing a singing inside it that your matchless eyes and ears have clarified.

Thank you, Kiki Smith, for your astonishing art.

Not without the Davis Mountains, horizon line of the Edwards Plateau, and Wild Horse Desert.

Not without my constant feline companion Linus, who guarded these pages by sitting on them.

Not without the love of my parents, Jason and Joan Fry, and my sister Sarah Ayala. You are my reason and my rhyme.

Finalmente, not without Julio Barrientos, el amor imprevisto de mi vida, who shelters my heart in the harbor of his. This book chronicles my before, pero el próximo es tuyo. Y a todos los Barrientos: gracias por dejarme ser parte de tu familia.

For my parents, who never gave up the ghost of hope that the prodigal son would find his way home—

Vespers

Was my song a feathered thing?—
How sing the sharp wing unbroken
When my mouth is broken wing?—

—Dan Beachy-Quick

credo

like a preacher's son returned to God
—but never the church—

hungover from afternoon's endless
lesson in thirst—I do not know

where I am going or how this late
July—below the eye of Sirius

rabid & bright—I pray you find me
near the strung out corner of Babcock & Prue

where the carne asada smells especially spicy
tonight—since sky's enamel lid slammed shut

I've looked for that angel unawares,
prodigal or pilgrim, saint or sinner, to ask

                    *

is body the shape of soul—
is soul the shape of body—

when, doubting, he touched to see
seeking the exact location

of soul's shining kingdom
of heaven behind spear-split skin

did Thomas find its aleph—
did Mary feel any pain

when crowning she
pushed out godhead

—Judas kissed Jesus
—did Christ kiss him back

breath on a coal

soul become flesh
you set it on fire

uncomfortable bones
your ancestors gave

hair for a shirt
bird for a heart

cinders of some star
unnamed you glow by

being breathed upon
are you this ember

or are you breath
(but whose breath)

debris field

in the agony of an eleven-year-old
afternoon,
            storm clouds blacken

180°, gunmetal rim
              of San Angelo horizon, foretelling
twister weather or, God-willing, rain

                    & hope
scant as cloud-covered 4pm
when hallway nightlights begin to blink

a half-remembered psalm,
              childhood left
you thumbmarked, open

            lilies
by the reservoir
a choir of husks

desert hymn
ghost tongue
        who's begun to speak

update after the possession

take the beast out of the boy
                    for bastard substitute

son mend broken
             with tongue

I'm afraid
           touched is as touched was

fact
       people are people

a man a man
            lost no longer

doesn't mean belong
              once strange always

estranged
         as marked is marked

awake or asleep
           Legion said no more

of its terrible things
              cloven hooves cliff-driven

unclean now clean again
                called by name

animals shy away
           even they remember

voices in my voice
           flies in my mouth

abomination buzzed
             should such sin live

singular again I wasn't

ever not an other

forgiven but unforgotten
                echo chambered walker

those who hear can barely
                meet my gaze

as if one eye's green
              & the other's brown

not-psalm 121

how we'd lifted burnt
offerings, our hearts. as shorn

           things bleat, cling. for help
           had not come. for our

bramble-bloodied feet
slipped—He slept—

           shadowed by absence of
           outstretched, His hand could

stave neither solar nor
oxidized green flares

           of moonglare watching over us,
           insomniac. we knew not

why the slow subtraction (devil's
arithmetic) of our right wrist

           bones clamored, cold,
           but who were we

heavy-laden looking for, Lord
where smoke risen from

           a ram's scapula was its lampblack
           psalm. to the hills we lifted

our eyes, threadbare antiphons.
deserts away from where we were

           promised benediction, our goodbyes
           blackened our altars. help had not come.

after

fledgling flown—or fallen from
hailstoned, the birdhouse

        shaped like a church

sparrows nested twine
in twists   sweetgrass

        bladed: wind sheared

rapture past thunder
stormed the backyard

        detonating dandelions, nettles

bereft of head: needled
heart violet

        star gone gray

update after the resurrection

because the body betrays
                               I called mine Judas

after he who kissed Christ
                               queer or so I'm told

did not recognize this
                               skin I was in as mine

what a funny thing flesh
                               I already told you

couldn't remember where I was
                               as any kind of *where*

even *still* was still
                               until & then it wasn't

light didn't light
                               zero whatsoever flared

color's candle gone
                               out then suddenly turned on

metaphor yes but true
                               see I told you it's tricky

because it never happened
                               before someone called something

sounds like a name
                               every shade coalesced

Lazarus a lightening
                               like mist I swirled around

it *hurt* I think
                               hurt the word I startled

because someone started

               weeping I heard *sisters*

yes called Mary called Martha
                    they tell me he wept

as I opened that's right my
                eyes said *brother* are you

there there they often
                 ask me where I am

looking at what shore
                  what world at where I was

Jesus their bright
              I held their yes

faces with *hands* beheld
                  was beckoned to the evening

meal laid out in honor
                of my being raised up

barely knowing the *table*
                  for the table it was

bread as bread & the *salt*
                as salt in my mouth

sloshed what's it called
                wine between teeth & tongue

unsure if I should laugh
                 or sob to once more be ensouled

beside the gardening he
                 who passed past strange

who let the leaf of me
                 undream frond from seed again

torn from a book of what happened

as a child I wonder-worried how the dead could see—

wherever my great-grandmother had flown

—so often the living close their eyes

is the character for heart literally written where light touches the face

＊

this is how the past begins.

to know not only what was, but the shadow of *who*.

mist between trees hung like sheets on a line.

sigils seen (fire throughout the woods) as if through a veil.

if *flame* did not, would *river* signify.

if not *stone*, would *spirit*.

as the Magdalene waits for his second coming

not one Mary but three

                    faces of longing legends

call me harlot penitent that one

                who weeps because he

was (understand) my shepherd

                   who set me on this righteous path

between his knees (yes) an altar

               where his anointing head

crowned mine with oil

                  (you'd call that blasphemy

as if you could ever know

             because you weren't there)

before he left I tasted

                  I saw my Lord was good

my mouth a cup spilling over

             with him the enemy other men

(who thought they understood)

                (who thought they loved)

(who thought that he)

watched us feast in the valley

of the shadows of his death

I could not bring myself to believe

when he said that my spirit will

be with you "always" while I'll

dwell in the father's house "forever"

preparing a place of honor

for you (sweet nothings any other man would say)

for if the light of the world is the world

without his warmth it wasn't

rather a desert I wander after

original desert mother & father

Galilee Egypt Ephesus Provence

all's wilderness so where doesn't matter

between always & forever I await

my beauty hallowed to a hollow

gristle & bone wind instrument

trust me when I tell you

whatever King David claimed

"I shall not want"

that philandering psalmist lied

my hair remembers exactly

not just the feet I perfumed

but every rising falling inch of him

why else do you think it drags the ground

what else but want could clothe me now

pilgrim

I was walking when
there was this edge

that was a problem:
words went missing &

dressed in sackcloth & ashes
I needed more than a gust

of God—in wind
blown upon—to believe

in more than a word
like loneliness was

I this hole in the
(dancing inside my chest

where no one saw)
heart do you still

shine in the dark
did you want

to be found
I fell in

nightwalk

[tell us our failings & if we're home]

though lovelier is easier
to see—   who would've

thought castawayed things
shipwrecked on the sad

sandspit strewn with drift
wooden spars   an alphabet

—that lost sang like this
(saltwater inside the eye)

[now I ache at the strange]

to dearest Him who lives
alas! away: bitter would have me

taste: my taste was me
—but worse, was gall, was heart

burnt, the radiographer said.
(if only answers were alkaline.)

gnosticism had eaten cleanly
through the esophageal lining

of my eschatology: x-rayed
raw from cigarettes & battery acid

sold as coffee at cornerstores.
handed a cup of clay, he

bade me drink   —but even novenas
can't coat a stomach already gone

firebox as the sun in its fifth cycle
—& just as dark matter may

be where God grew lonely—
HearestThou, can you

follow this ion trail
I am breathing: a chalkline

circle around my mouth

[now that we're lost at last]

whispers someone or thing
inside: fell of dark

before, resurrected, days
climb under the city of no

hills   sans serif
save for the crooked

mesquite patience
that built a Babel

skyward—   thunder drums
heaven's sheet metal veil

asunder   lightning's pentecostal
& tongued   already our words

were furrow-flung
seeds asleep among flint

(Bible broke open)
bedrock dreamt dragon

teeth   paleolithic arrowheads
floodwater, remembering, finds

Compline

You've got to start walking again
As what you have become
Since childhood put you in relation
To star, road, rotation.

—Fanny Howe

debris field

before the world darkened
                              you'd already
memorized the Alpha & Omega

                                        shadows tattooed
verses engraved upon
                        skin, in your

beginning there was right
& there is
              wrong, all that

is clean
            & what is not
of the Father

              just as he who lies
with a man as a woman shall
surely be put to death

                              whosoever liveth with these
scars shall dwell outside the camp
                                    where there is keen

there is keening
                    throat-wild howls
where such creatures are

                    never spoken of
you
stalk across the steppes

antiphon (preacher's son)

not writ but voice
graven on stone   flame-spoken
                    fact on flesh

iron finger
jealous God   inner eyelid
                  —nailed there

as Thomas—because he doubted—believed

        where you would
place your hands

      searching for a scar

        where the raiment
ripped (call it skin)

      open wound a mouth

        that cannot shut
God's silence shed

      his pierced side

        parable incarnate torn
here sundered from after

      word from flesh unmade

        (call it soul)
because I didn't then

      recognize this man

        who held out his arms
as the man I knew I loved

      (call it covenant)

        so I placed my hands there
where hurt was holy

      where belief meant nails

        to feel the invisible again
my wonder-stricken eyes made

      visible I reached for him

      past *verily*

beyond *I say*

    into *unto you*

debris field

                    & was this also given
for you, the loneliness of limestone's
                          memory of water

carried always, a handful of salt
                         saved from the city that burned
having already eaten, having drunk deep of

unleavened bread
sacramental wine
          &, also, a needle

to see through, thread
               for touch
only what's held in one hand

                  strands
of hair, your
          sorrow sewn into

a shirt
       as penitents
wear sackcloth & ashes

                  absence inside
an absence arisen, little Lazarus
walk in your shoes of fire

as Isaac upon the altar

—but, father, there is no other
obedient brother willing to

bare his throat
(shy swan)

where edged
belief-as-bronze

gone sharp
—father if you're

not Abraham, you
have no other son—

wilderness rose as incense

godliness stopped chasing us after hyssop was no longer found.

      smoke, suddenly, misspelled.

now no more than a crooked few.

          scattered like the teeth of lions long extinct.

absent thunder, memories lightning through us crossing snowmelt's streams.

      water falling on rock the only almost-human voice.

sift of pine needles, a music the elderly remember, but barely.

         —before he hardened into *he*.

read about but never before seen.

      before she softened into—

as if listening for a landscape beyond us.

        a boy ago, a girl.

in the book, it was written we would know we had arrived when we arrived.

diptych (his hairshirt)

but what does a god lack?

overheard in the ex voto

church-dark: cassock's tatter

unpolished chapel quiet

Our Lady of the Ashes unvisited

& a brink of dream dimly remembered

ragged, its never-mended hem: or, a passage

chosen by dowsing rod, the illuminated

page opened impromptu, prophesying

we shall not all sleep   wilderness

a god lacks only lack

voices cry out   *but we shall*

all be changed   gargoyle choir

chanting to the swallow congregation

—truesilver sometimes lies—

no monsters here but a candlelit

monstrance only a heretic adores

& the most blessed sacrament no more

than memory's aftertaste of

reliquary bones in which restless

revenants linger like Autumn

leaves swept from the narthex, unshriven

I blew the candle out

I blew the candle out
not knowing you had

gone out,
you'd gone—

＊

Santa Maria   that as I said
the words   Madre de Dios
votive flicker-lit
ruega por nosotros   Guadalupe's quickening
wick slendered   (yours silvered)

＊

ahora y en la hora

smoke risen like minutes

de nuestra muerte

leaden hour, your

＊

—ashes to ashes now,
dust to dust

for to dust we shall return
—returned, is your body

like anything here
there, that homeplace

grandmother star
where grandmothers go

when they die—
when you died

I blew the candle out
(your last breath)

I didn't know that
you'd let (we let) you go

there are four angels standing at the four corners of the earth

sometimes our hearts are animals

I cradled the cinders
by the waters of Big Joshua Creek

in both hands   barely alight, what had been

my mind: I'd heard
he was one of those boys

who air out their insides on windowsills

*

it had something to do with religion

every full moon, a choir of elderly monks
sing tone-deaf liturgies for each hour

for the virgin hair daily set on fire

inside the almost-ivory chapel,
my ribs an empty sparrow's cage

"had you not followed the vatic

*

your face," he'd said, "would have been

of brilliant countenance":   lithographic
landscape beyond the forgotten

ocean of the innermost ear

where one boy, with a wolf for a heart, wants
to eat the songbird nesting inside the other

it had something to do with religion

               *

when I tried to tell you every day's a seraph's four faces watching over

boy/bird   wolf/boy
you brought me the blessed earthenware

cup of winter spiked with nettles & nard

& not even the star dying in my mouth could
dull the bright draught's ashen rime

as Judas fleeing from the storm in his marrow

in the olive-adorned hour

before I betray you, already consecrated
                              your breath fills my mouth

as the first word animated

father-fashioned river clay,
                            when I kissed you, a sun

rose where your logos had been

wine-pressed words (*I am the vine*)
                            ripening the barren branch I'd become

*

—it was as if my tongue rusted

like the nail hammering
                         your severed sinew & bone

no more than a redolent hour before

Gethsemane, in the cypress
                         agony of God-with-us

don't tell me you didn't know

(*truly I tell you*)
                         sunset bleeds through the tree-line

disciple faces began to dim

when I ate of—
                         when I drank from (*forgive him*

*

Father, he knows not

what he does)
                              I know what I did

        shattered the moon—

my lips brought the gall
                        soaked sponge, its bitter herbs

        I'd swear even then

before the bread—your body
                        was broken, before cups

        of blood, yours shed—

thirty shekels bitten shards
                        of heaven illumined

        by the alephs of your eyes

Christ, what I tasted bled

nightwalk

[through leaves which naturally dizzied &]

psalms spun on
stems, dropped   from our

mouths spilled stone
syllables   seed fruits

rotten on the ground.
He who dwells in the shadow

of the Almighty   we saw
no sign save a raven

whose black beak   *[selah]*
pecked & pecked our prayers

[I don't need oceans to move myself over stones]

all these fossils we
held had glittered, swam

this diluvium where
glisten was once

crushed stone flecks
of river earth & sky

silver clasped   horns of Ammon
phylum Echinodermata   diatom

glint between our teeth (salt
so far inland on our hands, our knees

[open my heart for the night, it's empty]

slammed shut   sky
spoke only ragged

scraps of cloud   a scapular
for our frostbitten fingers

beneath nailbright stars
whose incisive light our teeth

even when we couldn't see felt
moths wending toward no moon

Vigils

Who is that in the space where your
self and your self do not meet?

—Kazim Ali

by the light of no moon

it's time, she said, for you to go
though you do not know this star-spare road

seated at the feet of the eldest
wisewoman tree, I tied

saffron thread to her oldest branch

for the breath's
quicksilver *who*

am I in the quiet bell
between inhale & exile

even though I do not know

how to leave ashes behind
this star-spare road remembers

embers awake
on the tongue

wrecked, solitary, there

—after Kazim Ali

when heaven's cracked bell

hung heavy around your neck
being lost or not belonging

did its silent clang have a name

not the desert without

but the sand inside your
scraped out inscape

being but an ear, some strange race

not *spirit-* but devil-ridden

was it grace that such sin should live
better for bones to finish knowing in air

when you wander, a burning cloud

seared between earth & sky

mind gone *numb*
you *intended to starve*

where there was *no lantern, no cup*

whisper where this was

tonight I need to ask why
does daylight's slit-wristed

fade always feel like dying

dear damn element of blank

utterly unmistakable ether
God how did you not plummet

will shining be spilled

if *paradise lies*

between a book's pages
beneath a mother's feet

scripture or rupture

was it written you asked

henna calligraphied on
your face *unwilling*

swirls unable to tell

despite all the ways to die

infinite as lines on your hand
in & out, compassion

you began to breathe

sun-spindled, stardust

in & out of you
Babel's son, brother dancer

syllable & sound

antiphon (gnostic stranger)

not dirt   not rain
in the book of names

serifs shaped like seraphim
ink dancing   black fire

on white fire spelled
where can I flee from

souls to be saved
your face   indecipherable

written in dirt
by rain rendered

illegible every letter
wingless my name

true north

dear drop of light spilled across 3 am
sky asleep in the heart of the bear
you are asking again September questions
only the shine of your siblings long fallen

ago in an embered age on earth
before the first fingers traced you
painted you in ochre & charcoal
oracle on rock & skin & bone

of the dead your even more ancient
orbit alone knows the answer to
how could flickering you have known
a sieve slept in the little of your dipper

almost invisible homesick eye
faraway your wandering lullaby

wayfaring

winter solstice
    like a shipwreck
        I foundered beyond

           any bell's quicksilver
    dip knee-deep

  year's longest night

before said light
    of this world
        woke up again

           —listening with
    my whole skin—

  not to self

but its unsaid
    penumbra felt
        like a body's

           shadow lantern
    shine behind

  no, inside—

the boat beached
    far from water's
        starlit soothsaying—

           sky's black branches
    dogwood dark

  bare & hands

against the prow
    (yesterday
        so much rain)

whose oars are

ready

as Eve, remembering Eden

world, it is always dusk—
in the beginning, every nightfall
was bright as the very first
dawn—only a child could
now hope to witness
flaming the sword between me

*

& my origin   —not that I would ever want,
even if I could go back   —yes, it's true,
when history began, stars were so near
we gathered them like fruit
from the vine, can you even imagine
—I had no need for memory

*

& I am not sure
if I can explain
what happened after

—before the word was
made flesh, the word
was flesh—   before *star*

*

was seen   before *tree*
was climbed   before *serpent*
was whispered   before *fruit*
was plucked   before *skin*
was naked   before *ashamed*

was cast into the garden, we

*

who had once touched what words
refer to grew apart, scattered
like seeds fallen on dry ground,
& our footprints filled with blood
where they littered the scorching sand,
mine first when the birth pangs began

*

soon followed by my firstborn's
soles stained red forever after killing Abel
—& as every wound has its corresponding word,
 I thought mine the mouth of grief   until generations after
Adam's missing rib returned to dust   through the women's eyes
I watched Mary watch her son's chest heave one last

*

time, in the Place of the Skull, stood still
—as when Cain's hands first brought violence into
the world—   then began to gush again
after the centurion withdrew his spear
& I caught a glimpse of it   Eden inside that gash
inviting us, children lost from the womb, to crawl in

you ghost in the logos

where is the first wood
                      cut in the ageless scroll

                              unrolling from so wide open
          a vanishing point (whose

etching is it) in its worlding we
                      call it time because the word is

                              not possibly world enough to
       begin by describing the beginning

(whose ink-stained hand
                    is it) this spirit all around us

                          released by sound we
         call time only an unfurling

end nowhere in sight
                    as in the beginning it was

as Jonah, hours into the third night, wondered

measure the horizon this not-night,

    not-sky but spine. as if the ribs were

        sextants no longer searching for even faint glimmers

      of some star other than the star-shaped disc

of the hole that, neither sun nor moon, never moves.

make even smaller fires of the

    hulks once ships. write every man

      who's ever failed you

    who you, also, failed. tell them

  that there's more than soil—

in sadness, all's ocean, but you can depend on

  salt's steadfast refrain. what water left you—

      a day as whole as a single grace note,

    that field you remember

  like the skin of your mother's face.

how you found some fires

  burn even underwater. & everyone

    who forgot, barnacles on their bones.

felt its echolocation. nostalgic for green's

  you've never seen the bottom but have

ghost, what leaves promise.

  that roots have also known this dark—

Advent, again

—*after Jean Valentine*

I still don't know how
to think of/with you

God-with-us

as many named as leaves
curled, Emmanuel, like ears

listening in my backyard

every branch bare
this tintype night

*

& your pregnant
mother word heavy
(swollen ankles, back pain,
stretch marks, heartburn)

& the hobbled
possum carrying young on her back
(her one lame leg)

& living & dead those
I love present, absent
(here-with-me)

& the least of those

& then the least of them

& how all their names, spoken, break
broken syllables of your name

& this world, Lord

*

this world   overcast
seventy-degree December
amniotic sky when

asleep did you think
of us   (how can a lamb
think of us)

                    *

where not all hours ring
bright   some burn blue
below Lady Bird Lake

& as if in said shadow of
we are walking in the darkness
of your face, Mary

inside valleys of Joseph's
worry   if every city is
Bethlehem on the solstice

road   angels   donkey   star
grandmother shepherded dark who
named your child mother father

yes who
called you
child light

nightwalk

[roads end where only trees greet them]

your edgelit answer, visible
only by the isosceles

of our asking   faint binary
star behind its brighter

unsaid shadow, cast from
not far, but nearer dark matter's

though its murmur does not speak
nor can we say whether

sanctuary's spectrum shifted
red or why   we felt it so,

belief being blue.   great-horned
owls gave up their evening

angelus, but the particle/wave of
paradox was parallax—

everyone's origin   self-same—
but the lines drawn on

our palms promised we'd
wander before we see to see

[tucked in the notch of my fossil-bones]

was a worry   that the crooked
outline I inhabit

was no more than a photo
gravure of a one-winged

sparrow—not the bird
but its inked intaglio

copper-plated feather
etchings audible on

spirit-colored paper, flapping
inside-outside my skin

[that crash we call a city]

one by one   then two
by two we fled under

cloud-cover   Advent
it's always a tabernacle

laved by the sweat of our brows
in the presence of *take, eat*

our ecclesiastics intoned
—even their censers sang

here, drink   but we didn't
could not   Lord they wanted our adoration

but we'd been faithful & faraway
You, Lord, were nigh

Lauds

Blessed are they who remember
that what they now have they once longed for.

—Jean Valentine

as the woman who grasped the hem of his garment

was the no name   woman who bleeds
was unclean they said   claimed they the law

twelve years nonstop   ran red as the Nile
cursed between my legs   wound where nothing

but dark came in   ruined my fortune
wasted on charms cures   everything manmade failed

how could I not   having heard go see if
this God-made-man   could make me hale

breathless among the throng   his eyes so ancient so new
whirled like wind around   who touched my robe

his disciple flock didn't   no but he did
had felt something   kneeling I cried Lord

somehow I knew that   if I could just
even the threadbare   dirt-covered ends

not even the physical fact   of his uncut nails
his miraculous hands   that had set the lame

walking again   who'd cast out the demon Legion
yes these wondrous tales had crossed   even my outcast ears

Cana wedding water into wine   the poor young man
he wept for dead   whose name Lazarus

sounded like lightning   left the grave
after one spoken word   lives again to tell

& I knew if I could   clutch only the least
dirtiest part of   his well-worn & traveled clothes

unwashed homespun   even without seeing
his face without even   hearing his voice

my hand reached out   unsure if I could bear it
if he looked at me   not sure that I could stand

if he didn't see   I was utterly without
hope if he would not   *Adonai* if he could not

but he knelt beside   he held onto & saw
shame scarlet streaked   I couldn't hide

because you believed   that you would be healed
said this more-than-man   as if my whole body a bell

behold my beloved   Daughter, Daughter you have been

how do you explain it

birdwings like brushstrokes.

shadow of heaven there are still times.

a voice said in no dream.

if the stars outnumber the dead.

early morning sky I am almost convinced.

though the heart can be blown out.

night's wreckage dawn's always.

some people actually inhabit their bodies.

as Lazarus risen like a blossom from bone

called by name
at the end
of my suffering there
was no door

but there was
a way if
it sounds terrible
to survive

(conscious)
buried in
dark earth
small mercy

I knew not
what trembling
souls most fear
to be entombed

in this body
unable to speak
you who can but
barely remember

being born in the
name of the voice
I rose up I
rose up again

swaddled for the under
passage from the other
world makes us
infants all

***

after four days grave
stench clung
a shroud

all around
no within
this corpse

grew lighter
as the voice
called my name

cairn stones
loudly sleeping
shook awake awake

commanded by he
whose word
for light was

light whose
breath poured
waters before

there were waters
murmuring deep
before water or light

how could I but obey
not a command
but a hand stretched

through the seventh
gate after gate
shades staggered

past forests of mist
shadow mutterings
on the river I didn't know

**

I'd been can you
tell me who

leaf deaf I am
blind as a cloud

before was dim
& if I like

a rain lily sprung from
ground why were the dead

no more than bones
dreaming of others

still dead & those
that could speak did

morning cut as night
had been a blanket once

when he breathed
his breath into my

lungs body throat
coughed dust desiccated

eyes salt stung
a veil wrapped around

what had been my
face another life

*

it was another

life my face

toward the cave

mouth rang lit

felt like fire

mine opened to

name his voice

was calling Lazarus

Lazarus come out

my hands became

my hands again

my feet my feet

veiled crossed between

never before & not yet

burned the threshold

my name foreign

as resurrection strange word

no dead man's tongue

soul, paraphrased

I have forgotten the word I wanted to say—

*

the waterwheel is still
waiting for river's song

*

prayer's tarnished
chalice couldn't hold

night's
spill, sky

*

—but I have forgotten the word I wanted to say

*

after fireweed blighted the wheat
field long fallow, whisper
sunrise, touch me

*

something understood—

*

tendril, leaf be green

as Mary after the eclipse of her radiance threshold

thus far, sunrise had always been

quiet, my time to spin
while I watched morning's
shutter, light

wefts crisscrossing the warp of the floor's packed dirt.

distaff & spindle.
tabernacle thread
chosen, dyed from the deep

insides of murex shells, Tyrian purple,

wool woven
finer than an infant's hair
unlike any other before

I saw he who was God's strength

(no, that's not right
not a he
as a man is

a man, no, not quite) as almost a girl.

as I was, still
that bird-boned.
that delicate.

before any feathers brushed the dusk of my hair

hushed, he stood in
my doorway, whispering.
& yes, I heard all

uncountable wings of his mouth pressed to my

trembling (maybe I imagined
but I'd swear he'd
never before trembled yet was).

how else explain blindsight eyes, why this

piece of sky—
hand outstretched—
lily pollen crown—

as stamen touched pistil, my spinning stopped.

Be it done unto me
I said, overshadowed by
his fear behind his *Fear not*

—quickening—*The Lord is with thee*

approximately never

would I have thought   if thought were prayer
any ever might find me   sure as a sparrow

        begging at the temple
        gate called beautiful

kneeling, here, again   between inhale &
exile, & also with   you, Lord

        a part of this circle
        made by our hands

held above the altar   not in prayer
but as prayer   for, as altar when

        Emmanuel
        —my original wound

word made flesh—   come near from far
my first kiss   God-with-us, here

        I am beggared by your
        beautiful, at your temple gate

antiphon (queer angel)

father earth
mother sky   for you, I'm still
                        waiting: the little girl

who died inside
of the little boy's   heart: you've held
                        her, in me, all this time

credo

say I am: otherwise agnostic, a believer
only when in unison
words are sung-said
beside another, stranger or
familiar, not alone

                —nonsense, maybe, but
if it's a symbol, to hell with it—

      grace looks like

      bread, wine, we

as Samuel in the temple

if I am here, Lord   (I am

here, Lord)   a little one-winged
—a drab brown sparrow,

yes—
under the stone

split wooden ledge, listening for
where   (are You, Lord?)

ever, lasting, You are—

wonder thicket

& after the wonders of the thicket
I was lost in had been
wandered, words were

no longer signs arrowing errantly
nailed to branches easily broken.
simple to say, but this geometry was

no frail wish. the sigils still spelled
sometimes aslant, others crazily, but the river
water sang clear, tasted true.

that night—every painstakingly wrought
knot of an Our Father come undone
—a rosary made of thorns

instead of thread woven between my fingers
like a ladder even Jacob could not climb.
above, tattered swatches of tree-tangled

sky looked stitched together, though I remembered
it always, always wheels. I woke as if
I hadn't slept an hour, yet I knew

in this wilderness the wildest things were
not without. but, within, the fire made from
kindling had watched the deepening dark

as long as it could keep both burning
eyes open, coals no more than ashes
best left behind. *all things that are—*

I wrote in soot on stone—*are lights*
without knowing why, listened to the morning birds
because dusk can never hope to see past its clouds

of unknowing. once, I only believed in
how flammable the smallest sorrows are.
& I don't know when, or how, but the peregrine

wind nested inside the thicket
I'd been walking through, its branches
beginning to whisper. I don't know what

they spoke of. something like *look, there
is a clearing*, & there was
a clearing &, further, a field

where there were no prodigals—
only other pilgrims—bewildered as I was,
as I am by the juniper in the air.

every time you wish the sky was something happening to your heart

as if it had something to do with
religion: spirit in the wheel
of cattle egrets spun
out of the scorched field
lonely for livestock, eyes
of the alfalfa still asleep
below the saltpan moon
—even if the gloaming wells up from this

hallowed ground   *I will not let thee go*

Jacob's pillow   *except thou*

white feather ladder   *bless me*

I think there is no light in the world
but the world

And I think there is light

—George Oppen

Notes

Borrowed, echoed, remixed, or inverted, the following authors' words walk beside my own:

At Vespers, the lectionary reading comes from Beachy-Quick's "North/South Composition."

"breath on a coal" echoes the ending of Jean Valentine's "Home."

"torn from a book of what happened" refracts a line of Carolyn Forché's "The Garden Shukkei-en."

"as the Magdalene waits for his second coming" is inspired by Donatello's *Penitent Magdalene*, Kiki Smith's *Mary Magdalene*, and the apocryphal legends that begin where gospel accounts end. Dedicated, because of her own poems about the Magdalene, to Jill Alexander Essbaum.

The titles of each "nightwalk" poem quote poems by Fanny Howe. The series dialogues with, and is an homage to, her work.

"[now I ache at the strange]" repurposes language from Hopkins's "I wake and feel the fell of dark, not day." "HearestThou" is John Felstiner's translation of Paul Celan's neologism *Hörstdu*, a word for the divine found in Celan's "Conversation in the Mountains."

At Compline, the lectionary reading comes from Howe's "Forty Days."

The italicized language of "debris field [before the world darkened]" quotes Leviticus 13:46 from an unknown translation used as an epigraph to James L. White's *The Salt Ecstasies*.

The title of "wilderness rose as incense" quotes Kerri Webster's poem "Atomic Clock."

"diptych (his hairshirt)'s" subtitles come from Beachy-Quick's "The Laurel Crown"; it quotes 1 Corinthians 15:51.

"I blew the candle out" is for my maternal grandmother, Velma Young Bryant.

The title "there are four angels standing at the four corners of the earth" and the poem's italicized phrases come from Brigit Pegeen Kelly's "Three Cows the Moon."

The title "as Judas fleeing from the storm in his marrow" repurposes a phrase from Ellen Hinsey's "On the Uncountable Nature of Things."

"[through leaves which naturally dizzied &]" quotes Psalm 91.

At Vigils, the lectionary reading comes from Ali's "Math."

"by the light of no moon" borrows the wisewoman tree from Valentine's "The branches."

By way of Emily Dickinson's "I Felt a Funeral, in my Brain," "wrecked, solitary, there" dialogues with the work of Kazim Ali and is dedicated to him. Italicized language draws from Ali's *The Far Mosque*, *The Fortieth Day*, and *Bright Felon*; Jane Cooper's "Waiting"; and Dickinson's "The Brain – is wider than the Sky –."

"antiphon (gnostic stranger)" quotes Psalm 139.

The theory of language espoused in "as Eve, remembering Eden" owes an imaginative debt to Eve Grubin's essay "After Eden: The Veil as a Conduit to the Internal."

"Advent, again" responds to Valentine's "December 21st" and is dedicated to her.

"[roads end where only trees greet them]" adapts language from Christina Davis's "The Raven's Book" and Dickinson's "I heard a Fly buzz – when I died –."

At Lauds, the lectionary reading comes from the title poem of Valentine's *The River at Wolf*.

"how do you explain it" quotes "If You Are Asked" by Olena Kalytiak Davis.

"as Lazarus risen like a blossom from bone's" beginning echoes Louise Glück's "The Wild Iris."

"soul, paraphrased" adapts language from George Herbert's "Prayer (I)." It also borrows from Osip Mandelstam's "I have forgotten the word I wanted to say," translated by Clarence Brown and W.S. Merwin.

"as Mary after the eclipse of her radiance threshold" owes an imaginative debt to Mary Szybist's Marian poems.

"credo [say I am]" quotes an observation of Flannery O'Connor's about the Eucharist from a letter collected in *The Habit of Being*.

"approximately never" draws on Acts 3. Dedicated to Alex Darling-Raabe, Chris Darling-Raabe, Shawn Hampton, everyone affiliated with Table of Mercy, and the Paulist fathers at UT-Austin's University Catholic Center.

"wonder thicket" quotes Johannes Scotus Eriugena and Kathleen Peirce's "Regret." This poem is dedicated to her.

The title of "every time you wish the sky was something happening to your heart" is a quotation from Kalytiak Davis's "A Few Words For The Visitor In The Parlor."

The closing epigraph comes from Oppen's "The Poem."

ABOUT THE AUTHOR

John Fry received an AB in English from Davidson College in North Carolina and an MFA in Poetry from Texas State University-San Marcos. He is the author of the chapbook silt will swirl (New Border, 2012). His poems have appeared or are forthcoming in *Colorado Review, West Branch, Blackbird, Waxwing, Denver Quarterly, Devil's Lake,* and *Third Coast,* among other places, as well as in the anthologies *New Border Voices* (Texas A&M UP, 2014) and *Imaniman*: Poets Writing in the *Anzaldúan Borderlands* (Aunt Lute, 2016). Fry is currently a poetry editor for *Newfound Journal* and a doctoral candidate at the University of Texas at Austin, where he is writing a dissertation on medieval English literature. Originally from South Tejas, he lives in the Texas Hill Country.